Railways of Asia
South Korea and Taiwan

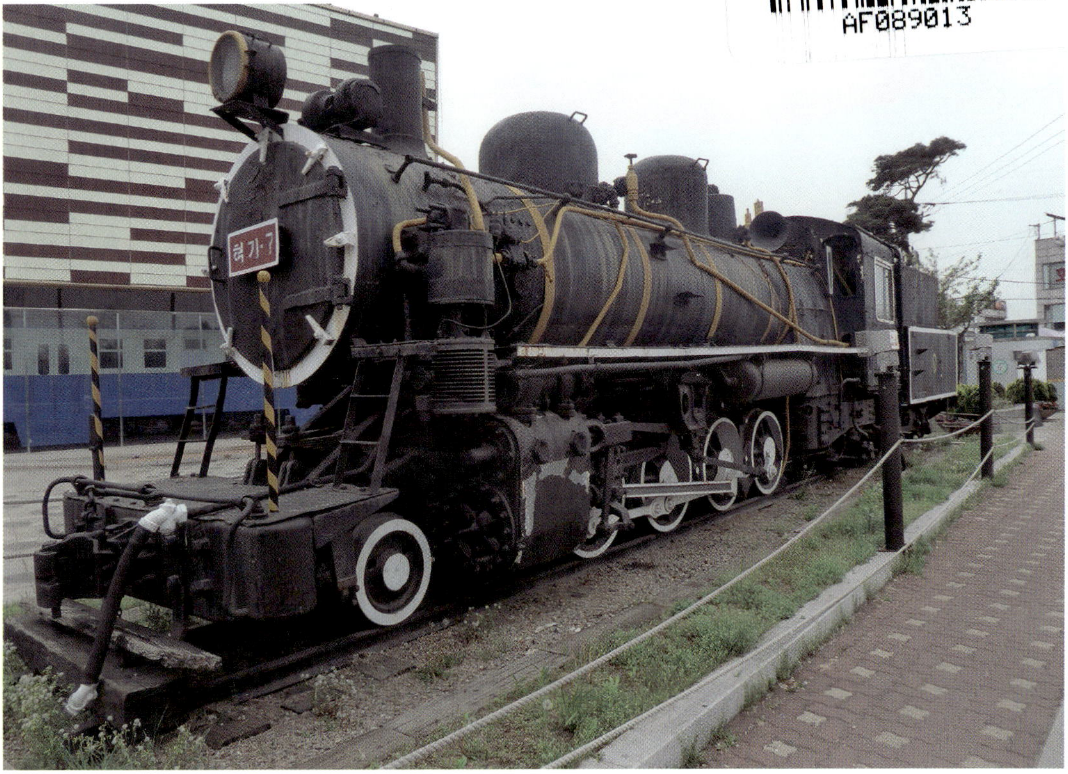

DAVE SPOONLEY

Key Books

WORLD RAILWAYS SERIES, VOLUME 8

Front cover image: Alishan Railway, 4 October 2015.

Title page image: Suin Line Locomotive No 7, Sorae History Museum, South Korea, 23 April 2019.

Contents page image: Chiayi station, Taiwan, 4 October 2015. Electric Locomotive E210 arrives with a special train.

Back cover image: Kaohsiung station, 16 March 2013. E232 stands in the station. Since this photo was taken, the tracks have now been diverted into the new underground station.

Published by Key Books
An imprint of Key Publishing Ltd
PO Box 100
Stamford
Lincs PE9 1XQ

www.keypublishing.com

The right of Dave Spoonley to be identified as the author of this book has been asserted in accordance with the Copyright, Designs and Patents Act 1988 Sections 77 and 78.

Copyright © Dave Spoonley, 2023

ISBN 978 1 80282 639 5

All rights reserved. Reproduction in whole or in part in any form whatsoever or by any means is strictly prohibited without the prior permission of the Publisher.

Typeset by SJmagic DESIGN SERVICES, India.

Contents

Foreword 4

Part 1 – South Korea
Chapter 1   Introduction to South Korea 5
Chapter 2   Metropolitan Seoul 7
Chapter 3   Incheon 20
Chapter 4   The Demilitarized Zone 26
Chapter 5   Gangneung and the East Coast 30
Chapter 6   Mokpo 35
Chapter 7   Daegu 38
Chapter 8   Busan 41

Part 2 – Taiwan
Chapter 9   Introduction to Taiwan 45
Chapter 10 Taipei and Taoyuan 47
Chapter 11 Hsinchu 52
Chapter 12 Chiayi and Alishan 55
Chapter 13 Kaohsiung 71
Chapter 14 Hualien 79
Chapter 15 Pingxi 85
Chapter 16 Taiwan High-Speed Rail 92

Bibliography 95

Foreword

This book is a sequel to my two-part series about Japan's railways, and covers two of Southeast Asia's lesser-visited countries, South Korea and Taiwan.

During the early 20th century, both were ruled by Japan, Korea (as it then was) being a Japanese protectorate from 1905 and a colony from 1910. Taiwan was ceded to Japan after a war with China in 1895. Both remained under Japanese rule until 1945.

While railway development in both countries had commenced before the Japanese occupation, it was under Japanese rule that the networks of each were developed to near the extent we see today. More recently, both of them have developed high-speed railways and urban rapid-transit systems.

One of the things I enjoy in travel is finding hidden links and connections. In this book, the connection between the locomotive at Sorae, south of Incheon, South Korea, and LDT103 at Hualien, Taiwan is one such link.

This book is neither intended to be a definitive history of the two countries' railways, nor is it a travel guide to either country, but it serves as a photographic record of my travels around these lesser visited Asian countries. I hope it will encourage readers to make similar visits.

The author at Imjingang station, near the Demilitarized Zone, South Korea, 2019.

Part 1 – South Korea

Chapter 1
Introduction to South Korea

A brief history of South Korea's railways
South Korea's first railway opened between Seoul and Incheon in 1899, relatively late in the history of railway development. In 1898, the Korean government awarded a contract to a Japanese company to build a line between Seoul and Busan. This line opened in 1905. Following Japan's occupation of Korea in 1910, development of the network increased.

Gangneung station, 26 April 2019. A Mugunghwa service stands at Gangneung headed by Korail 8256.

To ease congestion between Seoul and Busan in the modern era, the government proceeded with South Korea's first high-speed railway. In 1989, enquiries were sent to Japan, France and Germany, the most prominent high-speed operators at the time, and the resulting line, constructed between 2004 and 2010, is based upon French TGV technology.

South Korean railway gauges

Originally part of a greater Asian railway system including China, most railways in South Korea are standard gauge. There also existed a small number of 2ft 6in narrow gauge lines, which have now closed.

Train services in South Korea

The main train operator in South Korea is Korea Railroad Corporation, which operates under the Korail name. Korail operates the following services:

1. High speed, or Korea Train Express (KTX) services; these are operated by either KTX-I trains, based upon French TGV Réseau trains, or KTX-Sancheon trains.
2. Classic line services, operated as either ITX-Saemaeul services (the fastest services on classic lines), or Mugunghwa services (slower but still with limited stops).
3. Dedicated tourist services, the availability of which tends to ebb and flow with time. At the time of my visit, these included the DMZ train, the Seatrain and the O train.

In 2016, a new private operator started services on the Seoul to Busan and Mokpo lines. Super Rapid Train (SRT) operates out of Suseo station in eastern Seoul.

Rapid Transit

Currently rapid transit systems operate in the following centres:

- Seoul Capital Area – 23 lines
- Busan – 6 lines
- Daegu – 3 lines
- Daejeon – 1 line
- Gwangju – 1 line

Train travel in South Korea

Train travel in South Korea is easy and safe. On my visit, I purchased tickets required from ticket offices. The staff are helpful and generally speak English. It helps to pre-research which train you wish to travel on, and arrive with it written down. The website www.letskorail.com has a good search facility. Korail also offer a rail pass.

For rapid transit systems, a T-Money card can be purchased at many stations and is usable on transit systems throughout the country.

Chapter 2

Metropolitan Seoul

Seoul has been the capital of Korea since the 14th century and, since the Korean War (1950–53), the capital of South Korea. Today the city has a population of nearly 10 million and is a thoroughly modern Asian city with a vibrant cultural scene. It also has a fine collection of historical buildings and palaces.

In addition, there is an 18.6km long city wall surrounding the old city. Approximately 80 per cent of the wall is still complete and walking the walls is an interesting, albeit strenuous walk. There is one small section in the north of the city that is in a military zone. You have to present ID to enter this section and it is closed on Mondays. In many places the gates in the wall removed during the Japanese occupation have been reconstructed.

Seoul is a major centre on the South Korean railway system with frequent departures, both regular and high-speed, to all corners of the country.

Line 1 of the Seoul Metropolitan Subway opened in 1974. Since then, the network has expanded to 23 lines with 768 stations. In the outer suburbs, the subway trains run along the Korail tracks.

Old Seoul station, 19 April 2019. This station building opened in 1925 and closed in 1988 when the new station to the left of the former premises opened. The old station bears an uncanny resemblance to the old Luzern station in Switzerland. In 2011, the former station reopened as a cultural centre, and its restored interior is well worth a visit.

Old Seoul station, 19 April 2019. The 1988-built station, with its associated Lotte department store, can be seen to the left of Old Seoul station. In the foreground is a former highway flyover repurposed as an elevated pedestrian walkway, complete with food stands and no fewer than six pianos.

Seoul station, 19 April 2019. Viewed from the pedestrian walkway, a Mugunghwa train is arriving at the station from the Susaek Yards to the north. The train is hauled by a Korail Class 8200 locomotive; these are part of the Siemens Euro Sprinter family of locomotives.

Seoul station, 21 April 2019. The curved concourse has steps and escalators to access the platforms to the left of this view. Further to the left is the ticket office, and the wooden structure above the concourse is the first-class lounge.

Seoul station, 21 April 2019. Down the stairs are the main platforms. From left to right can be seen a KTX-I train, a KTX-Sancheon and two further KTX-I trains.

Seoul station, 21 April 2019. A KTX-Sancheon arrives from the north. These trains were built by Hyundai Rotem and entered service from 2010.

Seoul station, 21 April 2019. A Mugunghwa train headed by Class 8200 8246 awaits departure from Platform 7.

Seoul station, 21 April 2019. A northbound oil train headed by Korail Class 8500 8509 comes through Platform 12. The Korail Class 8500 electric locomotives were built in 2012–14 by Hyundai Rotem and Toshiba.

Seoul station, 26 April 2019. In the foreground, a KTX-I train awaits departure. These trains are based upon French TGV Réseaux and the first 12 were built by Alstom in France between 1997 and 2000. The remaining 34 sets were built in South Korea by Hyundai Rotem between 2000 and 2002. In the background is a Class 7300 diesel, 7348, on another oil train. These locomotives were built by EMD.

Susaek Yards, 22 April 2019. Susaek is one of the main yards in the Seoul area. Here, various Mugunghwa train sets await their next duties.

Susaek Yards, 22 April 2019. Freight trains at Susaek Yards.

Susaek Yards, 22 April 2019. EMB-built 7462 at Susaek Yards. The archway-shaped structure behind the locomotive was built to protect locomotives during the Korean War.

O-Train, 24 April 2019. The O-Train operated between 2013 and 2020 on a loop from Seoul, the journey taking about five hours. Each car of the converted Korail Class 200000 four-car train had a specially designed interior. Here 200852 awaits departure from Seoul.

O-Train, 24 April 2019. O-Train interior showing 'couple rooms'.

O-Train, 24 April 2019. O-Train interior café area, complete with coloured glass ceiling.

U-Line, 20 April 2019. The U-line is an 11.3km-long driverless light rail system operating in Uijongbu City to the northeast of Seoul. Opened in 2012, it has had a chequered history, with its original promoter filing for bankruptcy in 2016. The line has an interchange with Seoul Metropolitan Subway Line 1 at Hoeryong and later crosses the Subway again near Gangeung station. The U-line is operated with 15 Siemens VAL 208 units.

U-Line, 20 April 2019. Train interior.

U-Line, 20 April 2019. Units passing at an intermediate station.

U-Line, 20 April 2019. Station U124, Songsan, is one station from the line's terminus at Tapseok.

Seoul Metropolitan Subway Line 1 at Ganeung station, 20 April 2019. Northbound train arriving. The lines through the station have been elevated to eliminate several level crossings.

Soyosan station, 20 April 2019. Soyosan became the northern terminus of Seoul Metropolitan Subway Line 1 when the line was extended in 2006. The Gyeongwon Line continues north from Soyosan to Baengmagoji near the Demilitarized Zone. Prior to the Korean War, the line used to continue further northwards into what is now North Korea. A DMZ train started running from Seoul to Baengmagoji via Soyosan in 2014 and was suspended in April 2019 to allow for the upgrading and electrification of the Gyeongwon Line north of Soyosan.

Soyosan station, 20 April 2019. At a level crossing immediately south of Soyosan station, a Seoul Metropolitan Subway Line 1 returns south to Seoul.

Seoul City Walls, Namsan Oreumi Elevator, 22 April 2019. Installed in 2009, this could be South Korea's only funicular and is only 63m long.

Seoul City Walls,
Namsan Oreumi Elevator,
22 April 2019.

Seoul City Walls,
22 April 2019. Some parts of the city walls are on inaccessible steep ground. To assist the stonemasons in their repair and reconstruction work, rack monorails transported the material for use on the trickier locations.

Seoul City Walls,
22 April 2019. The temporary monorail line snakes through the trees.

Chapter 3
Incheon

In 1883, Incheon was the first place in Korea to open up to trade with the outside world. Today, the city still offers an interesting collection of historical buildings in its Open Port and Chinatown areas.

Incheon was also the western terminus of Korea's first railway, opened in 1899 between Seoul and Incheon. This line is currently used by the trains of Seoul Metropolitan Subway Line 1, the journey from Seoul taking about 70 minutes. Line 1 trains started running in 1974. In addition to the services on the Seoul Metropolitan Subway, Incheon has its own two-line subway system, operated by the Incheon Transit Corporation.

Incheon was also the terminus of the 2ft 6in-gauge Suin Line, the name being an abbreviated version of Suwon-Incheon. This line opened in 1937 and served the then-predominantly agricultural area between Suwon and Incheon. The narrow-gauge line was progressively closed, with the last trains running in 1995, though a number of important relics of the narrow-gauge line still exist in the area.

The successor to the narrow-gauge Suin Line is the standard-gauge Suin-Bundang Line of the Seoul Metropolitan Subway. This line opened progressively between 2012 and 2020.

Incheon station, 23 April 2019. Two trains of Seoul Metropolitan Subway Line 1 stand in the platforms.

Incheon station, 23 April 2019. Behind the two-storey main station building are located the tracks of Seoul Metropolitan Subway Line 1. Underground are the lines of the Suin-Bundang Line.

Wolmi Sea Train, 23 April 2019. Adjacent to Incheon station is the terminus of the Wolmi Sea Train. This line opened in October 2019 after a troubled construction. Originally this monorail was planned to have trains carrying up to 70 passengers. However, a poor safety record even before it opened forced the opening to be postponed indefinitely and the line was later reconfigured for smaller trains carrying 24 passengers. Here, one of the smaller trains is on a test run near Incheon station. Below the monorail are the electrified lines linking Incheon station and Incheon port.

Suin Line, 23 April 2019. Near Woninjae station on the Suin-Bundang Line is the former bridge that used to carry the narrow-gauge Suin Line across a creek.

Sorae History Museum, 23 April 2019. If you alight at Soraepogu station in Sorae City and walk towards the river, you will find the excellent Sorae History Museum. Outside the museum is Suin Line No 7, a 2-8-2 locomotive of Chosen Railway Class 900, which I believe was originally numbered 907. These locomotives are some of the largest 2-8-2 locomotives built for the 2ft 6in gauge. Fifteen of them were produced in the late 1930s and 1940s and another four were built for use in Taiwan. At least three other locomotives of this type are preserved in Korea.

Sorae, 23 April 2019. Viewed from the Sorae History Museum are the former narrow-gauge railway bridge across the river and the current Suin-Bundang Line Bridge.

Sorae History Museum, 23 April 2019. Inside the museum there is a whole area dedicated to the narrow-gauge Suin Line, which includes this replica of a car once used on the line.

Sorae History Museum, 23 April 2019. Interior of the same replica car.

Suin-Bundang Line, 23 April 2019. A train leaves Soraepogu station in Sorae City on the Suin-Bundang Line.

Suin-Bundang Line, 23 April 2019. Soraepogu station.

Suin-Bundang Line, 23 April 2019. Train interior.

Chapter 4
The Demilitarized Zone

Approximately 50km north of Seoul is the Demilitarized Zone (DMZ). This geopolitical anomaly has now existed for 70 years. In 1945, at the end of World War Two, a line was drawn across the Korean Peninsula following the 38th parallel (38°N). At the time, the only purpose of this line was to delineate the surrender of Japanese troops; the Soviets would accept the surrender of Japanese troops north of the line and the Americans would do likewise south of it. However, in reality, the 38th parallel soon become the frontline in the Cold War. During the Korean War, the front moved continuously, with Seoul changing hands four times. At the end of this war, the truce line lay approximately on the 38th parallel but wasn't entirely straight. It is now known as the Military Demarcation Line, and, on each side of it stands a 2km buffer from which both sides were to withdraw, known as the Demilitarized Zone. The South Korean side also has an additional area restricted to civilians.

Korail's Gyeongui Line links Seoul to the Demilitarized Zone. When opened in 1905, it formed the link between Seoul and Pyongyang, but the division of Korea in 1945 saw the line severed and following the Korean War, services north of Munsan were further suspended. Following a summit between the North and the South in 2000, the line has been progressively restored, a new bridge across the Imjin River being constructed and new stations built at Imjingang and Dorosan. This restored part of the Gyeongui Line, opened in 2002 with the hope that through trains between the North and the South would soon be restarted. Since then, however, little progress has been made with regards to

Near Seoul station, 21 April 2019. The DMZ train is a converted Korail Commuter Diesel Car, one of a batch built by Daewoo Heavy Industries between 1996 and 1999. The train used on the DMZ service has been specially altered for its use as a tourist excursion train, with special seating and a distinctive livery.

through trains. Dorosan station remains as a symbolic border station awaiting the arrival of through trains, and is the only station in the civilian-restricted area.

In 2014, two specially constructed DMZ trains started running. The western train operated from Seoul to Dorosan over the Gyeongui Line, while the eastern train operated from Seoul to Baengmagoji station via Soyosan over the Gyeongwon Line. Operations of both trains were suspended in 2019, the western train due to concerns of an outbreak of African swine fever and the eastern train to allow for upgrading of the Gyeongwon Line.

At the time of my visit in April 2014, the western DMZ train departed from Seoul station at 10.15 before arriving at Dorosan about an hour and a half later. The train then waited at Dorosan for the return journey that left mid-afternoon. While at Dorosan, it was possible to take a bus tour of the 'sights', which included the Dorosan Peace Park, the Dora Observatory and the Third Infiltration Tunnel.

Above: Seoul station, 21 April 2019. The DMZ train has arrived back at Seoul station.

Right: Seoul station, 21 April 2019. The DMZ train to Dorosan at 10.15 features among the more conventional departures on the information board.

DMZ train, 21 April 2019. DMZ train interior.

Imjin River Bridge, 21 April 2019. Viewed from the new bridge constructed between 2000 and 2002 is the former Gyeongui Line bridge over the Imjin River. The original bridge was destroyed during the Korean War. The southmost couple of spans have now been repurposed as a viewing platform to look northwards across the river, which marks the southern limit of the civilian-restricted area.

Above: Dorosan station, 21 April 2019. The DMZ train stands on the platform awaiting its return trip to Seoul. Note the extensive platforms provided at this border station, only used at the time by the three-car DMZ train.

Right: Dorosan station, 21 April 2019. Dorosan is the only station in the civilian-restricted area and opened in 2002. It is a fully equipped border station but, at the time of my visit, no-one was crossing the border. Following the suspension of the DMZ train in 2021, a new Gyeongui–Jungang shuttle service commenced between Imjingang and Dorosan.

Below: Dorosan station, 21 April 2019. Dorosan station interior.

Chapter 5

Gangneung and the East Coast

Gangneung is the largest city in Gangwon-do on the northeast coast of South Korea and is located approximately 100km south of the Demilitarized Zone.

Gangneung was used as the coastal venue during the Pyeongchang 2018 Winter Olympics and, for this reason, received substantial investment. This included a direct high-speed line to Seoul and the reconstruction of the station with new underground platforms and an approach tunnel. Prior to the construction of the high-speed Gangneung Line, all trains arrived at Gangneung on the Yeongdong Line from Donghae, along the coast to the south.

The reconstruction of the station and its approaches has left the former Yeongdong Line through the city as an interesting linear park.

South from Gangneung operates the Sea Train, another of Korail's tourist trains. This initially follows the Yeongdong Line to Donghae and then branches off onto the Samcheok Line to continue southwards along the coast.

Gangneung station, 24 April 2019. A KTX-Sancheon train awaits departure to Seoul. The underground platforms and associated tunnels, constructed in 2017, enabled Korail to eliminate a number of level crossings in Gangneung.

Gangneung station, 24 April 2019. Ascending from the platforms is a very fine modern circular concourse area.

Gangneung station, 24 April 2019. The 2017-built station exterior.

Namdae River Bridge, Gangneung, 24 April 2019. This bridge used to carry the Yeongdong Line across the Namdae River until this section of the line was bypassed in 2017.

Former Yeongdong Line, Gangneung, 25 April 2019. The former track bed of the Yeongdong Line through Gangneung has been imaginatively converted into a linear park, some of the features of which preserve the memory of the former railway.

Seatrain, Gangneung station, 25 April 2019. The Seatrain is another of Korail's tourist trains and operates along the Yeongdong Line and the Samcheok Line to Samcheok station. As with the DMZ train, the train is a specially converted Korail Commuter Diesel Car. The Seatrain livery features nautical themes, and many of the seats face sideways to offer the best views of the spectacular coastal scenery.

Seatrain, 25 April 2019. The interior of the Seatrain.

Samcheok station, 25 April 2019. The Seatrain has arrived at its terminus at Samcheok station, where it will lay over for several hours. This station is located adjacent to a huge cement works, which is a major source of freight on the Samcheok Line. While the train lays over, its passengers are free to explore the local coastal communities.

Samcheok Haebyeon station, 25 April 2019. I walked along the coast to Samcheok Haebyeon (Samcheok Beach) station, where I got back on the train to Gangneung.

Chapter 6
Mokpo

The high-speed lines south of Seoul split at Osong. The Gyongbu Line heads southeast via Daegu to Busan in the southeast of the country, and the Honam line heads southwest to terminate at Mokpo.

Located on a peninsula in the southwest of South Korea, Mokpo is literally at the end of the line for trains, and further transportation must be by sea.

Well worth a several-day visit, Mokpo is an historical port with several interesting attractions, including a large maritime museum.

Osong station, 28 April 2019. A station at Osong opened in 1921, with the current high-speed station opening in 2004 as an interchange between the Gyeongbu high-speed rail line and the Chungbuk Line. When the Honam high-speed line opened to Mokpo in 2015, Osong station became a high-speed line junction. Here a KTX-I train waits on the platform while a KTX-Sancheon train heads south, about to pass under the flying junction to the south of the station.

Mokpo station, 26 April 2019. Mokpo is the end of the line, and here two KTX-Sancheon trains line up facing the buffer stops. Whilst the current station is relatively modern, the Honam Line to Mokpo dates back to 1913.

Mokpo station, 27 April 2019. Awaiting their departures in this view from behind the buffer stops are a KTX-Sancheon train that will operate on the Honam high-speed line, and a slower Mugunghwa train that will operate via the classic Honam Line.

Mokpo station, 27 April 2019. An SRT (Super Rapid Train) awaits its departure. Owned by the SR Corporation, SRT started operating in 2016 and operates two routes from Suseo station in eastern Seoul to Mokpo and Busan.

Mokpo station, 27 April 2019. Korail Class 210000 trains were introduced in 2014 and marketed as ITX-Saemaeul services. These replaced the Saemaeul-ho services, which prior to the introduction of the KTX high speed trains, were the fastest trains in South Korea.

Mokpo station, 27 April 2019. A Korail 4400 Class locomotive is shunting in the yard. These locomotives were built by Hyundai Rotem in 2001.

Chapter 7
Daegu

Daegu is South Korea's fourth largest city and is sometimes called 'colourful Daegu'. Located on the Gyeongbu Line between Seoul and Busan, it is served by both KTX trains and Mugunghwa services. Gyeongbu Line services started calling at Daegu station in 1905. Daegu has two stations, Daegu and Dongdaegu (Daegu East), the latter being served by the KTX and SRT high-speed services.

The city also has a three-line metro. Standard-gauge Lines 1 and 2 opened in 1997 and 2005 respectively, while Line 3, opened in 2015, is a straddle-beam monorail 25km long with 30 stations.

Above: Daegu Metro Line 3, Myeongdeok station, 30 April 2019. A train arrives at the station, which forms the interchange with Daegu Metro Line 1.

Left: Daegu Metro Line 3, Myeongdeok station, 30 April 2019.

Daegu Metro Line 3, Chilgok Kyungpook National University Medical Center station, 30 April 2019. The monorail train has arrived at the terminus of Line 3 and has run into the centre line to prepare to change direction.

Daegu Metro Line 3, Daebonggyo Bridge, 30 April 2019. Line 3 crosses this impressive cable-stayed bridge.

Daegu Metro Line 3, Daebonggyo Bridge, 30 April 2019.

Dongdaegu station, 30 April 2019. The guard of an SRT train awaits departure to Suseo station in eastern Seoul.

Dongdaegu station, 30 April 2019. A KTX-I train arrives through the maze of overhead cables.

KTX-I train interior, 30 April 2019. This is Set 02, one of the original 12 sets built by Alstom in France.

Chapter 8

Busan

The port city of Busan is South Korea's second city, with a population of 3.6 million. The city also acts as the main gateway to southern Japan, with frequent ferry services to that country.

Railway-wise, Busan is at the southern end of the Gyeongbu Line and the Gyeongbu high-speed line from Seoul. Having enjoyed railway connections to the capital since 1905, Busan station was substantially rebuilt to accommodate the high-speed trains in 2010. Adjacent to Busan station is the ferry terminal.

Busan has a four-line metro system. Lines 1–3 opened in 1985, 1999 and 2005 respectively and are of conventional standard gauge. Line 4 is quite different, being an automatic rubber-tyred guided metro. In addition, there is the Busan Gimhae Light Rail Transit (BGL), which links Lines 2 and 3 to Gimhae International Airport. The Korail Donghae Line has also been upgraded to metro standards.

Busan station, 30 April 2019. Mugunghwa train No 1208, departing at 07.48 to Seoul, awaits its departure from Platform 3. This train will take about 5½ hours to reach Seoul, whereas the KTX service will cover the same distance in just over 2½ hours. The Mugunghwa services are used by travellers going shorter distances to stations not served by the KTX services, and by passengers on a budget.

Busan station, 30 April 2019. Interior of Mugunghwa train No 1206.

Busan station, 28 April 2019. Viewed from the footbridge linking the station to the ferry terminal, a KTX-I train approaches the platforms from the stabling sidings to take on passengers for its next service to Seoul.

Busan Metro Line 4, 29 April 2019. A train on this automatic rubber-tyred guided metro approaches an intermediate station.

Busan Gimhae Light Rail Transit (BGL), 29 April 2019. A two-car light rail vehicle comes out of the reversing sidings into the platform at Sasang station to commence its next service to Kaya University. The BGL opened in 2011 and is operated by a dedicated fleet of light rail vehicles built by Hyundai Rotem.

Donghae Line, 29 April 2019. In the Busan area, this line has been elevated on a concrete structure and improved to metro standards. Here a second generation Korail Class 381000 EMU calls at a station in the greater Busan area.

Donghae Line, 29 April 2019. Two Class 381000 EMUs on the Donghae Line. The left-hand train is a second-generation example built by Hyundai Rotem in 2018 and numbered in the 381X11–381X17 series. The right-hand train is a first-generation example new in 2016, also built by Hyundai Rotem and numbered in the 381X01–381X10 series.

Left: Beetle Ferry, 1 May 2019. The Beetle is a hydrofoil ferry service that operates between Fukuoka, Japan, and Busan, South Korea, and is operated by JR Kyushu. The journey takes about three hours and operates several times per day.

Below: Beetle Ferry, 1 May 2019. Ferry interior.

Part 2 – Taiwan

Chapter 9
Introduction to Taiwan

A brief history of Taiwan's railways
Taiwan's first railway opened in 1891 under China's Qing dynasty. Under the Japanese colonial government, the system expanded significantly so that in 1945 there was a continuous 3ft 6in-gauge railway from Su'ao, south-east of Taipei, to Fangliao, south of Kaohsiung. There was also an isolated 170km-long 2ft 6in-gauge line on the east coast.

Very few additional lines were built thereafter until the North Link Line opened in 1980, connecting Su'ao and Hualien. This was followed in 1982 by the regauging of the East Line from 2ft 6in to 3ft 6in gauge. Finally, in 1991 the South Link Line was finished, completing the rail loop around Taiwan.

Hualien station, 15 January 2013. EMD-built R100 class R114 stands at Hualien.

Electrification of the Western Trunk Line was completed in 1979. The North Link Line was electrified in 2000, the section of the East Line to Taitung in 2014 and the South Link Line is scheduled to be completed in 2024.

Taiwanese railway gauges

The main Taiwanese railway network is built to 3ft 6in gauge. The Taiwan High Speed Railway and the rapid transit systems use standard gauge.

The 2ft 6in narrow gauge lines are used for either logging, mining, or sugar cane railways.

Train services in Taiwan

The main train operator in Taiwan is the Taiwan Railways Administration, which operates the following services:

1. Classic line services: these are either fast or local trains.
2. Services on a number of branch lines mainly aimed at tourists.

High-speed services are separately operated by the Taiwan High Speed Railway.

Rapid Transit

Rapid-transit systems currently operate in the following centres:

- Taipei – 6 lines
- Taoyuan – 1 line
- Taichung – 1 line
- Kaohsiung – 2 lines and a Light Rail line

Train travel in Taiwan

Train travel in Taiwan is easy and safe. On my visits I just bought the tickets I needed from ticket offices, where the staff are helpful and generally speak English. It helps to research which train you wish to travel on and have it written down.

The website www.railway.gov.tw has a good search facility.

Chapter 10
Taipei and Taoyuan

Located at the northern tip of the island, Taipei is Taiwan's largest city, with a population of 2.6 million. Taoyuan is located southwest of Taipei and is the location of Taoyuan International Airport.

Taipei is a major railway terminus with fast and local services to the south along both coasts. The city also has a six-line metro system.

Taipei station, 11 January 2013. The current station dates from 1989, when the first stage of the Taipei Railway Underground Project was completed. Prior to this, trains used to pass through central Taipei on the level, causing a great deal of congestion. The station is served by Taiwan Rail Administration local and long-distance trains, Taiwan High Speed Rail trains and the Taipei Metro.

Taipei station, 11 January 2013. The station contains a large concourse area.

Metro Taipei, 11 January 2013. Since the first line's opening in 1996, the Taipei Metro has grown to a six-line network with more than 130 stations. All lines except the Wenhu Line operate on standard-gauge tracks. Here is a two-level interchange station, with the lines configured to allow as much cross-platform interchange as possible. At the time of my visit, the line on the right was operational, but the line which would use the platform located on the left was yet to commence operation and the platform was cordoned off.

Metro Taipei, 11 January 2013.

Metro Taipei, Zhongxiao Fuxing station, 10 October 2015. The Wenhu Line was opened in 1996 and was extended in 2009. It is different from the other metro lines in Taipei in that it is an automated rubber-tyred metro and is elevated in parts. Here an Innovia APM 256 train approaches Zhongxiao Fuxing station, which is the interchange with the Metro Taipei Bannan Line. These trains are the second generation to operate on the Wenhu Line and were introduced in 2009.

Metro Taipei, Taipei Zoo station, 10 October 2015. Taipei Zoo is the southern terminus of the Wenhu Line. Here a pair of VAL 256 trains leave the station for Taipei Nangang Exhibition Center terminus. The VAL 256 trains were introduced on the Wenhu Line upon its opening in 1996.

Taoyuan International Airport, 19 January 2013. Taoyuan International Airport is the main airport for Taipei and since 2017 has been connected to central Taipei by the Taiwan Taoyuan International Airport Mass Rapid Transit. The Taoyuan International Airport Skytrain, meanwhile, is a people mover that operates shuttle trains on two parallel tracks between the two terminals of the airport.

Taoyuan station, 3 October 2015. Taoyuan station is on the 3ft 6in-gauge classic line on the west coast of Taiwan. The station first opened in 1893 and was rebuilt in 2015, just before this photograph was taken. Here E1000 class loco 1045 brings up the rear of a push-pull set destined for Taipei. The E1000 locomotives were built in 1996–97 by Union Carriage & Wagon of South Africa with GEC-Alsthom electrical equipment.

Taoyuan station, 3 October 2015. A Series 500 EMU arrives with a southbound train. These trains operate local services throughout the electrified network and were constructed by Daewoo in 1995–97.

Series 500 EMU Interior, 3 October 2015.

Chapter 11
Hsinchu

Hsinchu is the oldest city in northern Taiwan and has a population of 390,000. The city is one hour's travel from Taipei on a fast train on the classic western trunk line, and an hour and a half travel by local train. In 2007, Hsinchu also gained a station on the Taiwan High Speed Railway; this station is located out of town and to get there it is necessary to take a shuttle train on the Liujia Line.

The Neiwan Line is 28km long and opened as far as Chutung in 1947 before being extended to Neiwan in 1951. The line was built to serve local cement plants and limestone mines, but today it operates a frequent service for tourists. In 2007, the first section of the line between Hsinchu and Zhuzhong was double tracked, electrified and level crossings removed in conjunction with the construction of the Liujia Line to serve Hsinchu HSR station. Since the opening of the Liujia Line, the majority of Neiwan trains operate from Zhuzhong to Neiwan.

Hsinchu station, 3 October 2015. Looking south, two Series 500 EMUs are on the right. In the shed in the distance is an E413 and a Diesel Rail Car (DRC).

Hsinchu station, 3 October 2015. The station building is a fine Japanese-era construction dating from 1913.

Zhuzhong station, 3 October 2015. DR1001 stands together with DR1017 at Zhuzhong station to form the service to Neiwan. The DR1000 trains were constructed in 1998 by Nippon Sharyo in Japan.

DR1001 interior, 3 October 2015. The DR1000 trains used on the Neiwan line have been specially adapted for the tourist service, with each train having its own theme.

Hexing station, 3 October 2015. Hexing is one of the intermediate stations on the Neiwan line.

Neiwan station, 3 October 2015. Neiwan is very popular with day trippers and boasts an interesting early-1950s station building.

Chapter 12
Chiayi and Alishan

The city of Chiayi lies about 100km north of Kaohsiung, Taiwan's second city, and has a population of approximately 275,000. Chiayi is about an hour north of Kaohsiung by fast train, or two hours by local train.

For the railway enthusiast, Chiayi is the gateway to the Alishan Railway, one of Taiwan's top attractions. Over a distance of 80km, the Alishan Railway climbs from Chiayi, at about 30m above sea level, to the mountain community of Alishan at about 2200m; most of this climb is achieved in about 60km. Along its journey, the line passes through the coastal plains, the tropical zone and the sub-tropical zone before reaching the temperate zone. In this zone grow cypress trees and it was to log and transport these trees that the railway was built.

With a track gauge of 2ft 6in, the railway was built by the Japanese between 1907 and 1912, with passenger and freight traffic starting in 1920. Although initially a logging town, Alishan has developed into a mountain resort and today is a major destination for visitors. Passing through mountain terrain, the railway has a number of spirals and zig-zags to assist it in gaining altitude. The same terrain renders the line prone to damage, particularly from typhoons. During Typhoon Morakat in 2009, the line suffered substantial damage and at the time of my first visit in early 2013 was closed, except for the shuttle trains operating from Alishan. By 2015 it was partially re-opened, and I was able to ride to Fenchihu, 46km from Chiayi. Full reopening is not expected before 2023.

At the time of my visit in 2015, trains departed Chiayi for Fenchihu at 09.00 and 10.00, with both trains laying over at Fenchihu before returning at 14.00 and 15.00; the journey each way took just over two hours.

The Alishan Railway is also famous for its Shay locomotives, the line having one of the largest fleets of these locomotives in the world. Eight 18-ton two-cylinder Shays were delivered between 1910 and 1913, and were obviously a success, as 12 larger 28-ton, three-cylinder Shays followed between 1912 and 1917. Many of these locomotives are still on the Alishan Railway. The line started experimenting with diesel traction in the 1920s, and from the 1950s successive batches of diesel locomotives have been delivered.

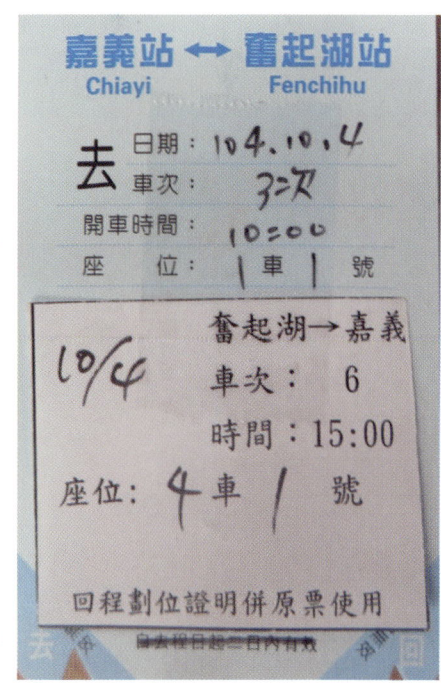

Today, typical passenger cars are about 10m long and, for safety, are propelled uphill by a locomotive at the downhill end. The cars on the Chiayi–Alishan service have forward-facing seats, while the cars used for shuttle services from Alishan have inward-facing bench seats, as the trips they operate are of short duration.

In Chiayi at Beimen is the railway's main workshop and depot, plus a large display of preserved locomotives and rolling stock. There is still an operational depot at Alishan.

Join us as we take a trip from Chaiyi to Fenchihu and visit the Alishan Railway operations at Alishan.

Chiayi station, 4 October 2015. Behind a sea of parked motorcycles is the main building of Chiayi station. The station opened in 1902, with the current building dating from 1933.

Chiayi station, 4 October 2015. A northbound local service operated by 563, a Series 500 EMU, pauses at Chiayi. The structure above the train is part of a canopied bridge that provides a pedestrian link from one side of the station to the other.

Chiayi station, 16 January 2013. A freight train consisting of boxcars heads south through the station.

Chiayi station, 4 October 2015. DL49 brings the cars that will form the 10.00 to Fenchihu into the Alishan Line platform at Chiayi. DL49 is one of a series of five locomotives (DL47–DL51) delivered by the Taiwan Rolling Stock Corporation, a subsidiary of Nippon Sharyo, in 2007.

Near Chiayi station, 4 October 2015. The 09.00 departure heads through the back streets of Chiayi, just after leaving the station. The train is operated from a driving position in the front car. Note the large number of pedestrian level crossings.

Beimen Depot, 4 October 2015. DL51 passes through the depot yard.

Beimen station, 4 October 2015. Beimen is 1.6km from Chiayi and is a major boarding point, particularly for coach parties. The station building dates from the opening of the line in 1912 and, although badly damaged by fire in 1998, is wonderfully preserved. Note the altitude plate (31m above sea level) by the corner of the station building.

Beimen station, 4 October 2015. In the sidings are four maintenance trains; note how each has a driving cab for propulsion uphill.

Beimen Depot, 18 January 2013. Between Alishan and Beimen stations is Beimen depot. As well as housing the line's main depot and workshops, it also features a museum of historical locomotives and rolling stock in well-landscaped grounds. Here is the operational train preparation area.

Beimen Depot, 18 January 2013. 28-ton Shays 25 and 26 were both built in 1914, and both apparently operational.

Beimen Depot, 16 January 2013. Viewed across the turntable, 28-ton Shay 23 is one year older than 25 and 26, dating from 1913, and is stored non-operational. Behind the locomotive is a rake of wooden-bodied coaches.

Beimen Depot, 16 January 2013. DL2 is one of the line's early diesel locomotives and is a six-wheel diesel-mechanical example supplied by Mitsubishi in 1953. Its long fixed wheelbase caused problems on the line's tight curves, so locomotives of this type were not purchased again.

Beimen Depot, 4 October 2015. DPC7 is a classic Alishan Railway diesel railcar. Following the success of two purchased from Nippon Sharyo in 1962, five more were purchased in 1966 and three further examples in 1970.

Beimen Depot, 16 January 2013. Interior of DPC railcar.

Beimen Depot, 18 January 2013. Old wooden-bodied car 39. These cars are sometimes used for special services hauled by the operational Shay locomotives.

Beimen Depot, 16 January 2013. DL37 is one of a batch of three locomotives (DL35–37) supplied by Orenstein & Koppel of West Germany in 1976–77. Poor relations with Japan at the time led to a boycott of that country's products, ruling out purchases from Nippon Sharyo, the railway's usual preferred supplier. While the German products were generally successful and up to the job, Orenstein & Koppel's requirement that spares had to be only purchased from them, and the high cost of these, forced the early demise of these locomotives. Once the boycott had been lifted, the railway returned to its usual supplier.

Above Zhuqi station, 4 October 2015. We now recommence our journey to Fenchihu; above Zhuqi station, the line leaves the coastal plain and begins to climb through the tropical zone. In this section are several 180° curves; here is the second, which also occurs on a level crossing.

Zhangnaoliao station, 4 October 2015. Between Zhangnaoliao (543m) and Dulishan (743m) the line negotiates a triple loop, involving ten tunnels, to gain height. Unfortunately, it looks more spectacular on the map than it is from the train, as most of the lineside scenery is thick forest. We are about to leave Zhangnaoliao station and enter the first tunnel.

Fenchihu station, 4 October 2015. We have now reached Fenchihu (1403m), 46km from Chiayi and DL51 and its five-car train awaits its departure at 1500 back to Chiayi.

Fenchihu station, 4 October 2015. Each car interior has 1+2 forward-facing seating and seats 25 passengers in air-conditioned comfort. Fortunately, on my journey to Fenchihu I had the one opening window in the car by my allocated seat, so was able to open it on occasions to take photographs.

Fenchihu station, 4 October 2015. High above Fenchihu are some interesting hiking trails with good views of the mountain town and the station. Both of the day's trains stand in the platform; one will depart at 14.00 and the other at 15.00. At the far (downhill) end of the station is the modern locomotive shed, while in the sidings is another maintenance train. The roof in the bottom left of the picture belongs to the historical locomotive shed, now a museum, with the main town to the left of that.

Fenchihu station, 4 October 2015. In the historical locomotive shed-turned-museum are 18-ton Shay 18 and 28-ton Shay 29, built in 1913 and 1914 respectively.

Alishan station, 18 April 2013. We skip the section of line that has been closed since 2009 and continue our tour at Alishan. From here three different services are operated along former logging lines of the Alishan Railway: Alishan to Zhaoping, Alishan to Shenmu (Sacred Tree) and the sunrise services from Alishan to the sunrise viewing area at Zushan. The former two lines operate 10–12 return services per day and the latter operates an intensive service in the early morning. Here the first train of the day is arriving at Alishan station from the depot.

Alishan station, 17 April 2013. DL43 is on the Shenmu (Sacred Tree) service. DL43 is the last of a batch of five locomotives constructed by Nippon Sharyo in 1982.

Alishan station, 17 April 2013. Car 8502 is one of a batch of 24 cars constructed in the 1990s for services operated from Alishan.

Alishan station, 17 April 2013. Car interior. Given the short journey times, and because sometimes the sunrise services can be very full, the cars have longitudinal bench seating.

Shenmu (Sacred Tree) station, 17 April 2013. The journey from Alishan only takes about seven minutes.

Shenmu (Sacred Tree) station, 17 April 2013.

Alishan, 18 April 2013. DL50 approaches a level crossing on the Alishan to Zhaoping service.

Alishan, 18 April 2013. DL50 again, on a service in the forest.

Alishan, Mianyue Line. 17 April 2013. Viewed across the valley from Alishan is the destroyed rock-fall shelter on the Mianyue (Monkey Rock) line. During the 1990s, the Alishan Railway was in the process of developing the Mianyue line as an additional attraction. This all came to a halt in 1999 when the line was severely damaged by an earthquake and so far, has proved too costly to repair.

Alishan, Mianyue Line. 17 April 2013. A closer view of the destroyed rock-fall shelter.

Chapter 13

Kaohsiung

Kaohsiung is Taiwan's second largest city and largest port, with a population of 1.5 million. The city is the southern terminus of the trains on the western trunk railway and the Taiwan High Speed Railway. Diesel trains also link the city to Taitung and Hualian on the East Coast.

Since 2008, Kaohsiung has had a two-line rapid-transit metro and, since 2016, a light rapid-transit system when the first part of the Circular Light Rail opened. The full circle is due to be completed in 2023.

The former Kaohsiungkang (Kaohsiung Port) station has an interesting open-air railway museum which is well worth a visit. Also of interest to the railway enthusiast is Taiwan Sugar Museum, with its preserved locomotives and shed.

Qiaotou station, 6 October 2015. E232 heads a northbound fast train through Qiaotou station, just north of Kaohsiung.

Kaohsiung station, 6 October 2015. R137 stands in the platform. This locomotive is one of a batch of R100 class locomotives supplied to Taiwan by EMD in 1969.

Kaohsiung station, 6 October 2015. A long train comprising three DR3100 three-car diesel multiple units arrives at Kaohsiung. At the time of my visits in 2013 and 2015, only the Kaohsiung to Taitung and Hualien sections of the mainline network had not been electrified. Electrification was completed on the Hualien to Taitung line in 2014 and will be completed between Taitung and Kaohsiung in 2024.

DR3100 Interior, 7 October 2015. These units were built by Nippon Sharyo in 1998.

Kaohsiung station, 6 October 2015. Kaohsiung station was redeveloped on a large new site between 1933 and 1941. Since 2002, work has been underway to reconstruct the station and its approaches underground. Since my visit in 2015, the underground platforms have been commissioned. Here an E1000 electric locomotive-powered push-pull set arrives at the surface station. The large site in the foreground is part of the works to build the new underground station.

Kaohsiung station, 5 October 2015. This is the Japanese-built station building of 1941 construction. In 2015, it was marooned in the middle of a construction site but I understand it will be preserved as part of the new station.

Hamasen Railway Cultural Park, 16 January 2013. This mostly open-air museum is located at the site of the former Kaohsiung station. Since 1941, the station has been named Kaohsiungkang (Kaohsiung Port) and is now closed. The former sidings are used to display preserved items of rolling stock. CT259 is an example of the Japanese National Railways C55 Class, which are known as the CT250 class in Taiwan. Between 1935 and 1937, 62 examples were produced for service in Japan (Class C55) and nine (Class CT250) for service in Taiwan. The last of the Taiwanese CT250 locomotives was retired in 1982 and two are preserved.

Hamasen Railway Cultural Park, 5 October 2015. DT609 is a member of the DT580 Class, which is another Japanese National Railways locomotive type built for use in Taiwan. In Japan, the locomotives are called the 9600 Class, and between 1913 and 1925 a total of 770 was constructed, 39 of which were for Taiwan.

Hamasen Railway Cultural Park, 5 October 2015. CK58 is a 2-6-2T locomotive, belonging to the CK50 class constructed in 1912.

Kaohsiung Metro, Formosa Boulevard station, 5 October 2015. Formosa Boulevard is the interchange station between the Red and Orange Lines. Its central feature is the dome of light, a 30m-diameter illuminated coloured-glass ceiling.

Kaohsiung Metro, Central Park station, 5 October 2015. Another stand-out station is Central Park on the Red Line. There is a large overhead roof over the escalators, with gardens alongside.

Kaohsiung Metro, Qiaotou station, 6 October 2015. This Red Line station is a typical elevated affair and is the nearest station to the Taiwan Sugar Museum.

Circular Light Rail, 5 October 2015. The first stage of Circular Light Rail, or Green Line as it is known, opened on 16 October 2015, just over a week after my visit. Here three light rail vehicles are on test; these are CAF Urbos vehicles and operate catenary-free.

Circular Light Rail, 6 October 2015. Stop C10, Glory Pier, is under construction.

Taiwan Sugar Museum, 6 October 2015. This is based in the former Qiaotou Sugar Factory and is in the same condition as the day it closed; you can wander around all the buildings. The factory also had a 2ft 6in-gauge railway system and this is the preserved locomotive shed.

Taiwan Sugar Museum, 6 October 2015. Taiwan Sugar Corporation 353 was supplied by Tubize of Belgium in 1948, along with another 45 of these locomotives. At its peak, the Taiwan Sugar Corporation operated 300km of lines, of which only a fraction remains. Up to 1982, some of the lines operated passenger services.

Taiwan Sugar Museum, 6 October 2015. While there is only one steam locomotive on the site, there are many diesel locomotives.

Chapter 14
Hualien

Hualien lies on the east coast of Taiwan and, with a population of 110,000, is this part of the island's largest city and its only significant port. Eastern Taiwan has traditionally been quite isolated from the rest of Taiwan due to formidable mountain ranges in the way of effective transport links. Hualien was only linked with the main Taiwanese railway system in 1980, when the North Link Line was opened.

Hualien is also the gateway to Taroko National Park, the central feature of which is a gorge through marble over 20km long and up to 500m deep. Toroko is well worth a visit.

The east coast of Taiwan is also interesting geographically, as there is a rift valley running parallel with the coast for about 180km between Hualien and Taitung. This valley marks the meeting point between the Eurasian and the Philippine tectonic plates. The coastal mountain ranges between the rift valley and the Pacific Ocean are the only part of Taiwan on the Philippine plate.

Railway-wise, a 2ft 6in-gauge public railway was opened south from Hualien 87km to Yuli between 1909 and 1917. A similar, although private line extended northwards from Taitung 42km to Guanshan and opened in 1919. The section to connect these two lines was constructed between 1921 and 1926. For nearly the next 60 years, the East Line operated very efficiently as a 170km-long narrow-gauge line, mostly with diesel railcars in the latter years.

With the completion of the North Link into Hualien, the East Line was converted to 3ft 6in gauge and realigned in many places in 1982. Today, there are still many relics of the former narrow-gauge line to be found, including both former terminus stations at Hualien and Taitung.

Hualien station, 15 January 2013. Locomotive LDT103 is displayed outside the current Hualien station. Originally numbered LD503, this is one of the largest locomotives to operate on the East Line and is one of four locomotives delivered by Nippon Sharyo, one in 1941 and three in 1942 (LD501–504). These are the same design of locomotive as the Chosen Railway Class 900 locomotives used by 2ft 6in-gauge lines in Korea. Three more such locomotives were manufactured in 1943 (LD505–507), but two were on a ship sunk in the war and the third was never shipped from Japan, being dispatched by the US Army to Korea at the end of the war.

Hualien Railway Cultural Park, 7 October 2015. Just under three years later, LDT103 has been relocated to the Hualien Railway Cultural Park, which is based at the former narrow-gauge line's Hualien station.

Taipei station, 10 October 2015. LDK58 and a 1957-built diesel passenger railcar, LDR2201, are preserved outside Taipei station. The railcar is in the traditional ivory/yellow colour used on the East Line. LDK58 is one of 13 similar locomotives supplied by various makers to the East Line between 1915 and 1938, and is one of four examples preserved.

Hualien, 7 October 2015. On examination of the street map of Hualien, the former route of the East Line can be seen in the street pattern curving off the current line to the Hualien Railway Cultural Park at the former station. The memory for the former line is recalled in the paving in the pedestrianised street.

Former Hualien Port Line, 7 October 2015. In 1939, a narrow-gauge branch line was built from the old Hualien station to the Port of Hualien. The port breakwaters were constructed between 1930 and 1939, and this bridge carried the port line across the Meilun River.

Hualien station, 15 January 2013. The current Hualien station opened in 1980 as the terminus for trains coming from the north via the North Link, and marked the southern limit of electric services at the time. With many services terminating here, the extensive station was a good place from which to watch trains. Here R62 pilots an E1000 push-pull set into the station; this was one of 52 similar R20 Class locomotives supplied by EMD to Taiwan between 1960 and 1966.

Hualien station, 13 January 2013. An E1000 push-pull set stands in the sidings, while R62 comes through the station with a freight train.

Hualien station, 10 October 2015. E239 stands at the station with what appears to be a special service.

Hualien station, 15 January 2013. A diesel multiple-unit of the DR2700 Series, which were built by the Tokyu Car corporation in 1966. These units were built for the Kuang Hua Hao express services on the Western Trunk Line and lasted in service until 2014.

Hualien station, 10 October 2015. This is a TEMU2000 train, introduced in 2013 to reduce journey times between Taipei and Hualien; it uses tilting technology to increase the running speed.

Above: Hualien Port Line, 8 October 2015. As part of the North Link project, a new line was provided into the Port of Hualien. E329 is at the port, with the 1930s-built breakwaters visible in the background.

Left: Xiangde Temple, Tienhsiang, 8 October 2015. At Tienhsiang in the Toroko National Park, this funicular provides goods access to the temple. Its gauge is unknown but is about 2ft 6in.

Chapter 15
Pingxi

The Pingxi Line is one of the more accessible of the branch lines now used by tourist trains, as well as being one of the prettier and more interesting ones.

To ride the branch, take the mainline from Taipei towards Hualien and alight at Ruifang station. From there, Pingxi Line trains depart frequently. The only ticketing available on the Pingxi Line is a day pass which, once purchased, allows you to hop on and off the trains as much as you want.

The Pingxi Valley enjoys abundant supplies of coal, with many mines. This particular valley had some of the last coal mines in Taiwan, but the final mine closed in 1997. The nearly 13km long branch was privately constructed and opened in 1921 to transport coal from the local mines to Taipei, before being purchased by the government in 1929. Join us on an interesting, albeit rather wet, journey on the Pingxi Line.

Right: Ruifang station, 12 January 2013. We've just arrived from Taipei and are waiting for the Pingxi train as a local train arrives. The train is a Series 500 EMU.

Ruifang station, 12 January 2013. Shunting tractors DL1102 and DL1031 wait by the goods shed.

Ruifang station, 12 January 2013. The Pingxi train has arrived and comprises a pair of two-car DR1000 diesel railcars, Nos 1014 and 1028.

DR1000 diesel railcar interior, 12 January 2013. Vinyl bench seats and lino flooring, ideal for a wet day in the Pingxi Valley.

Jingtong station, 12 January 2013. After about an hour we've just arrived at Jingtong, the terminus of the Pingxi Branch. To the right are the former coal bins. There is also a mining museum at Jingtong.

Jingtong station, 12 January 2013. This small and rather fine Japanese-era station building dates from 1929.

Pingxi station, 12 January 2013. One stop back down the line is Pingxi station.

Near Pingxi station, 12 January 2013. Train crossing Sankeng Creek near Pingxi station.

Lingjiao station, 12 January 2013. A train returning to Ruifang pauses at Lingjiao station. The stations are generally well presented with wonderful gardens.

Shifen station, 12 January 2013. Shifen is where the line's services pass.

Shifen Old Street, 12 January 2013. Here the line runs through the centre of the town. It is a local tradition to let off sky lanterns from the main street.

Shifen Old Street, 12 January 2013.

Shifen station, 12 January 2013. A train destined for Jingtong departs from Shifen station.

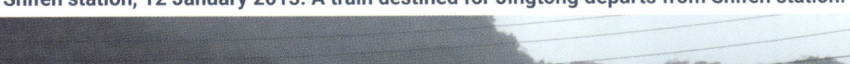

Chapter 16
Taiwan High-Speed Rail

After studies throughout the 1980s and 1990s, construction of a 350km-long high-speed line between Taipei and Kaohsiung began in 1998 and services started in 2007. At the time, this was the world's largest privately funded rail infrastructure project. Initially, ridership was low, which led to a restructuring of the promoter's finances being negotiated with the government.

One reason for the low ridership could be that the majority of the stations are at out-of-town locations, whose names are usually suffixed with 'HSR' for High-Speed Railway. The only station in the centre of a city is Taipei, as the high-speed trains use the tunnel through the city.

Since its opening, connections have been improved; for example, Taoyuan HSR station was initially linked to the airport by bus. However, since 2017, the Taoyuan Airport Mass Rapid Transit has taken over this task.

Initially services commenced with 30 12-car 700T trains, based upon the design of the Japanese Shinkansen Series 700 trains. Subsequently, between 2012 and 2015 a further four 700T trains have been delivered.

The maximum operating speed on the line is 300km/h. The fastest trains, with limited stops, take about 1¾ hours to travel the length of the line, with stopping trains having a journey time of 2 hours 25 minutes.

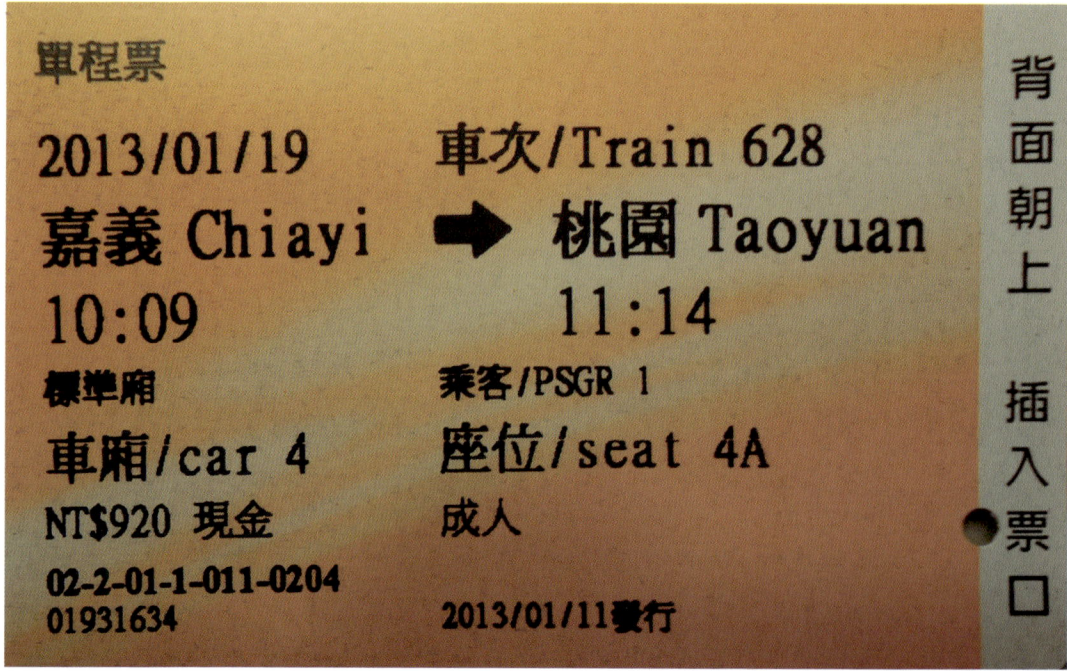

Chiayi HSR station, 19 January 2013. Northbound train 628 arrives at Chiayi HSR station at 10.09. Behind the fence on the left are the through lines for non-stop trains.

Chiayi HSR Station, 19 January 2013. 700T train interior. As with the Shinkansen Series 700 trains, the seating is arranged in a 3+2 arrangement and is reversible.

Zhuzhong station near Hsinchu, 3 October 2015. The Liujia line was constructed to provide access to the high-speed rail stations. In 2011, a 3km-long branch was opened off the Neiwan line to Liujia station, which is adjacent to Hsinchu HSR station, and frequent electric trains were introduced between Hsinchu and Liujia. Here a Series 600 EMU arrives at Zhuzhong station, with the high-speed line's viaduct in the background.

Zuoying station, 6 October 2016. Zuoying is the terminus of the high-speed line at Kaohsiung. To get to Kaohsiung from here, it is necessary to change to either the metro or the classic line services. Four 700T trains line up at Zuoying awaiting their next service northwards.

Bibliography

The following publications have been invaluable in compiling this book.

Name	Author/publisher
The Taiwan Railway 1966–1970	Loren Aandahl/self-published
The Taiwan Railway 1971–2002	Loren Aandahl/self-published
The Illustrated Handbook of Taiwan Railway Rolling Stock (Chinese text)	Su Chao-Hsu/Everyone Publishing
Narrow Gauge Railways of Taiwan, Sugar, Shays and Toil	Michael Reilly/Mainline and Maritime
Legend of Alishan Forest Railway through Hundred Years (Chinese text)	Su Chao-Hsu/Taiwan Forest Bureau
30-inch Railways Worldwide	David Scotney/Stenvalls
Taiwan	Lonely Planet guidebook

Other books you might like:

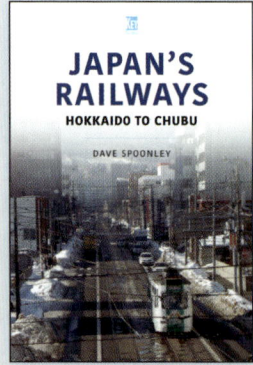
World Railways Series, Vol. 5

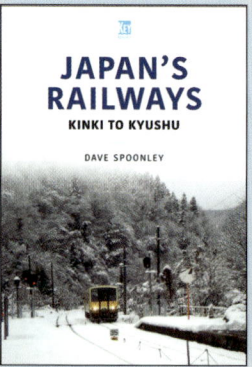
World Railways Series, Vol. 6

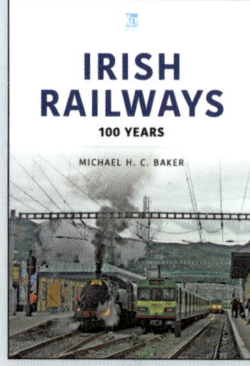
World Railways Series, Vol. 7

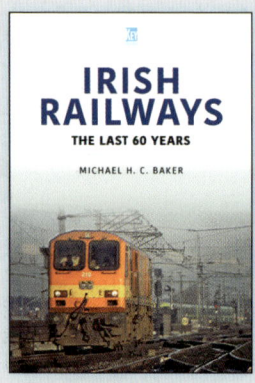
World Railways Series, Vol. 4

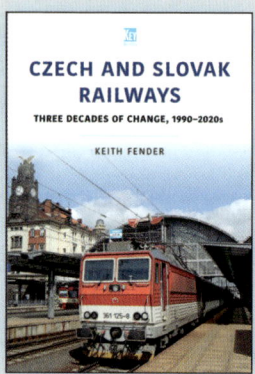
World Railways Series, Vol. 2

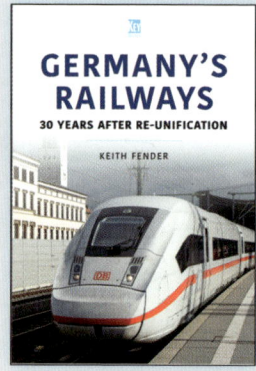
World Railways Series, Vol. 3

For our full range of titles please visit:
shop.keypublishing.com/books

VIP Book Club

Sign up today and receive
TWO FREE E-BOOKS

Be the first to find out about our forthcoming book releases and receive exclusive offers.

Register now at **keypublishing.com/vip-book-club**

Our VIP Book Club is a 100% spam-free zone, and we will never share your email with anyone else. You can read our full privacy policy at: privacy.keypublishing.com